THE ROMAN GARDEN

plants and gardens in Roman Britain

by

Michael Hoadley

FOR MY MOTHER

ACKNOWLEDGEMENT

The Roman Garden was written as a companion volume to my Roman Herbal.

In writing the present work, I consulted a number of works on Roman Britain and Gardening. These included THE CLASSIC HORTICULTURIST by Ursula Buchan and Nigel Colborn, FISHBOURNE: A ROMAN PALACE AND ITS GARDEN by Barry Cunliffe, HADRIAN'S WALL IN THE DAYS OF THE ROMANS by Ronald Embleton and Frank Graham, BRITANNIA by Sheppard Frere, ROMAN GARDENS by Marion Goodman, ROMAN VILLAS by David Johnston, LETTERS OF PLINY THE YOUNGER, NATURAL HISTORY by Pliny the Elder, ROMAN BRITAIN by I.A. Richmond, GARDENS ANCIENT AND MODERN by A.F. Sieveking, THE VILLAS OF PLINY THE YOUNGER by H.H. Tanzer, THE ARCHAEOLOGY OF GARDENS by Christopher Taylor, and THE HISTORY OF GARDENS by Christopher Thacker.

I am especially grateful to Frank Graham, the publisher of ROMAN HERBAL, for his encouragement and for the lively discussions we've had on the Romans and art and literature.

© 1996
Published by Frank Graham, Newcastle upon Tyne
I.S.B.N. 0 85983 143 4

Printed by
J. & P. Bealls Ltd., Bealim House, Gallowgate, Newcastle upon Tyne NE1 4SA

The Peristyle garden

In a Roman courtyard

INTRODUCTION

The earliest examples of ancient gardens come down to us from Egypt. In the temple and palace grounds along the fertile Nile banks decorative enclosed gardens flourished. Queen Hatshepsut had her new temple garden planted with incense trees. The use of decorative pots and planters for trees and shrubs became fashionable during the reign of Rameses III. In the tomb of Nebamon (c. 1400 BC) there is a painting of a well-stocked rectangular pool surrounded by fruit trees. The line and formality displayed in Egyptian gardens was later adopted by the Romans.

In about 600 BC at Babylon, terraces rising to a height of about 70 feet were landscaped and planted with trees and shrubs. These became known as the famous "Hanging Gardens". We do not know, with any certainty, where in the ruined city these were located, though two sites have been suggested. It is almost certain that the "Hanging Gardens" were rebuilt and re-landscaped several times in the history of the city.

The Assyrians collected plants for their temple gardens and the Persians developed the concept of the park.

We know that gardens flourished in the Mycenean Age, but few records of these remain. Sacred groves were maintained in Greece and on Crete. Homer gives us a description of the gardens of Alcinous, a legendary figure. In the Odyssey, he is represented as the King of the Phaeacians and lived on an island now identified as Corfu. The halls and gardens of his palace were regarded as exceptionally splendid.

The Lyceum in Athens had shaded public gardens. Today we would tend to regard these as examples of landscaping rather than gardening.

It is with the Romans that the concept of the formal garden as we know it developed. Their gardens drew on the past and on architecture for inspiration. The Romans brought the concept of the formal garden to Britain. This concept was to influence garden design from the 18th century to the present.

THE ROMAN GARDEN

Until the 1st century AD, Roman gardens were simple, informal affairs given over mainly to the growing of food. Then, the decorative garden became a popular feature of palaces, villas, and townhouses. Pathways provided a place for light exercise, and an evening walk before the main meal was considered beneficial to the digestion.

The Romans enjoyed outdoor living and they often furnished their gardens with as much care as they did the rooms of their houses.

The Roman formal garden was architectural in character. Flower beds and pathways were laid out geometrically. Fountains, statues, seats, and plant pots and troughs provided ornamentation. Trees were arranged in rows to repeat the rhythm of the columns and other architectural features of the building. Colonnaded walks provided shade or sun at different times of the day.

The garden was an extension of the house. Dining was often done in the open (alfresco), exercise was taken, worship was observed, and guests and visitors were received there. Fine linen curtains were hung outside to provide extra shade and imitate the household interior. Wreaths and garlands were hung on columns and architraves.

Ivy was extensively used. It was trained on walls and columns and formed 'swags' between columns and architraves in a formal design.

Formal hedging of box and rosemary was popular with the Romans. Planes and conifers were cultivated as ornamentals and were frequently used to make a feature.

Flower beds contained acanthus, violets, lilies, lavender, and roses as well as a great many herbs (see ROMAN HERBAL by Michael Hoadley). Rosemary, thyme, mint, coriander, rue, and hyssop added beauty and scent to the Roman garden. They also provided a store of plants for cooking and medicines.

The interior of the Roman house often reflected the love of gardens and the outdoors. Walls, floors, and ceilings were rustically decorated. Walls were painted with landscapes in the "trompe d'oeil" style.

The "four seasons" mosaic can be seen in the Corinium Museum at Cirencester. Only three of the roundels survive. Summer is represented by Ceres holding a sickle and with ears of corn in her hair. Autumn is Pomona in a headdress of fruit. Spring is Flora. Mosaics of Silenus, the god of hedonism, depict the vine. The vine was the symbol of wealth and prosperity.

Statues were a common feature of the Roman garden. Their display was a mark of respect and homage to the gods and ensured the

6

The Roman Garden was architectural in design and laid out in geometric patterns.

protection of the household. Venus was the guardian of gardens. Other statues were of gods and goddesses associated with fertility and growing things. These included Hercules, Diana, Mars, and Mercury.

The Romans ransacked Greece and its colonies for fine statuary. Vita Sackville-West (Collected Poems) described such a garden ornament: the statue of a vestal virgin.

"How slender, simple, shy, divinely chaste,
She wilting stood,
Her suppleness at pause, by leisure graced,
In robes archaic by the chisel woo'd..."

The less well off had to make do with Roman copies of Greek statues that were often of inferior quality.

Garden Temples and Shrines were common features of Roman landscaping

Small temples and shrines were often a feature of the garden. The Nymphaeum at Chedworth Roman Villa is a good example of this. The Nymphaeum, which was situated behind the bath house, was a water shrine. It was located on the site of the spring which fed the baths and had sacred, and possibly, healing associations. Water in all of its forms was a delight to the Romans. Their gardens frequently had fountains, pools, ponds, cascades, and even canals and rivers running through them.

Many gardens had elaborate underground watering systems. Fish ponds were popular. These were often decorated with aquatic mosaics. Water was frequently supplied to communities by means of the aquaduct.

In 1807, Dr John Lingard was the first to notice the remains of a remarkable aquaduct at Greatchesters on Hadrian's Wall: "...water for the station was brought by a winding aquaduct still visible from the head of Haltwhistle Burn. It winds five miles." Aquaducts are recorded in inscriptions from Chester-le-Street, South Shields, and Chesters. The channels of aquaducts have been identified at Bowes and Lanchester. Lincoln had a remarkable system made of tile pipes heavily jacketed in concrete: water was pumped up from springs. A gravity system carried below ground in timber pipes joined by iron collars provided fresh water to Caister by Norwich, Silchester, and Caerwent.

Citizens of the Roman Empire, who enjoyed an artificially high standard of living, did not have to trouble themselves with garden maintenance. This was done by slaves. Pliny wrote, "good husbandry goeth not all by much expense: but it is painstakingly and careful diligence that doth the deed."

A great deal of information about Roman gardens is to be found in the works of Pliny the Elder and Pliny the Younger. But it is doubtful that either of these urbane gentlemen ever lifted a hoe.

Pliny the Elder describes how a "toparius" could train planes and conifers into dwarf plants with a technique like the Japanese bonsai. Pliny the Younger describes his own villa gardens in detail in his letters. His villa in Tuscany had terraces which led to enclosed gardens. The gardens were designed to show their best aspects at all seasons. Box hedge alternated with laurel. There were grass lawns, beds of Acanthus, fruit trees and trellised vines.

Organic methods of fertilizing were the only ones available. Columella recommended the droppings of pigeons collected from dovecotes. However, the most successful manure was man's own. (Tomato plants found growing beside sewage works today are the result of seeds that have passed through man's digestive track.) Human

The Topiarius

excrement was sieved into a sort of a meal that, with the passage of time, lost "not only the stinking scent and ill-favoured sight that it had, but also turneth into a pleasant smell, and looketh lovely withal."

Corbridge Mausoleum may have been landscaped

THE KITCHEN GARDEN AND THE ORCHARD

Many town dwellers kept a "hortus" or small holding outside the town, just as people keep allotments today. But the villa urbana, townhouse, is unlikely to have had to depend too much on its own food production. The villa rustica, country house, would certainly have produced some, if not all, of its own food. As well as the associated farm, "kitchen gardens" would have been a common feature.

In Britain, the Romans introduced and cultivated carrots, peas, onions, leeks, asparagus, lettuce, radishes, turnips, and marrows. Apple, pear, and cherry trees graced their orchards and the grape was propagated.

The vine was almost certainly cultivated for its fruit and as an ornamental feature in gardens. However, there may not have been much wine production. The indigenous peasant population continued to drink beer: just as it had done before the conquest. Most, if not all of the wine, was imported.

During the 1st and 2nd centuries, extensive trade in wine was carried on with Spain. This jeopardized the position of Italian shippers so much that Domitian published an edict ordering the destruction of vinyards beyond the Alps. The edict had little effect and the 2nd century was marked by more and more viticulture in Gaul. Barrels made of silver fir found at Silchester are thought to represent the Bordeaux trade. If there were British vinyards, it cannot be said if their production was anything more than small scale for domestic consumption.

The ancient Britons ate wild apples (Malus pumila). They also made a type of cider from them. However, the Celtic apple was a small, hard, and bitter fruit. The Romans introduced a number of varieties.

The Romans developed distinct varieties of dessert apples. It is possible that one of these was Court Pendu Plat, which is still used in modern cross-breeding programmes.

Cato the Elder (234-149 BC) wrote a treatise on grafting. By the time of Pliny the Elder, there were more than 20 varieties under cultivation.

The wild pear (Pyrus communis) is also a hard and sour fruit. It grows as a small tree or shrub on the edges of woodland in southern Britain. It is ancestral to many dessert, cooking, and fermenting varieties. The flowers of the pear tree are particularly beautiful and give it a snow-covered appearance in the spring. For this reason, the pear tree makes an excellent ornamental in a formal garden. The wild cherry (Prunus avium) also bursts into white blossom in the spring.

Homer lists the pear as one of the fruits of Alcinous' garden. The

Romans developed improved varieties through grafting.

The history of the cherry is less well known than the apple or the pear: but its ancestry is thought to have been in Western Asia and Eastern Europe. Greek and Roman writers describe various varieties already widely spread before the time of Christ.

The apple, pear, and cherry were all cultivated en masse in orchards and were also used as isolated garden fixtures, just as they are today.

The gardens at Chedworth Villa

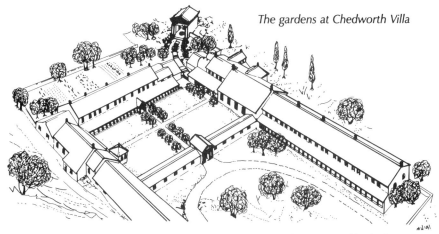

Chedworth Roman Villa, Gloucestershire, combined elements of both the courtyard and corridor styles of villa. The Nymphaeum can be seen at the top of the drawing. Kitchen garden and orchard are shown top left.

An ancient stone bridge with a statue of Britannia fronts the Italianate gardens at Iford Manor.

Garden Friends

Living Ornaments in a Roman Garden

Animal life was often important to the ornamental Roman garden: broadening the perceptions of sight and sound.

Aviaries were a feature of some Roman gardens. Birds were kept as pets for their gift of song and their powers of mimicry. Sparrows, goldfinches, ravens, crows, and blackbirds were all favourites. The mute swan ornamented garden ponds. The rarer black swan was highly prized. Juvenal (c. 60 - c. 130 AD) wrote, "a rare bird on this earth, like nothing so much as a black swan".

Pools and ponds were decorated with aquatic mosaics and well stocked with fish. One Roman Empress put her earrings on a fish in the palace pool. Mosaics of shells, a sea-god, and a dolphin survive from Verulamium.

In Britain, as elsewhere, the keeping of bees would certainly have been a feature of the villa farm. Honey was the principal sweetener of the Romans. It was used in many of the cooked dishes, whether sweet or sour. It was also used as a preservative and in medicines. Pliny says, "the honeyed wine is very nutritive and breedeth good flesh."

Virgil wrote a treatise on bee-keeping. He recommended that hives made from plaited osier wands or hollow bark should be placed near the flowers the bees prefer.

The "apiarius" was employed to tend the hives and there was a thriving commercial industry in the procurement of honey.

IN THE SERVICE OF THE DEAD

Flowers and plants have been associated with the honouring of the dead since Neanderthal times, 50,000 years ago. Neanderthal burials at Shanidar Cave in the Near East had been carpeted in flowers. It is therefore not surprising that more advanced cultures carried on the practice.

Roman tombs were often surrounded by gardens. Trimalchio, a wealthy freedman, gave precise instructions for the furbishment of his tomb. "It is to have a frontage of 100 feet and a depth of 200 feet, for I should like to have all kinds of fruit growing round my ashes, and plenty of vines." A banqueting hall was also provided.

Garden tombs had shaded dining areas (triclinia), fountains, statues, flower beds, and even a house for caretakers. Two or three gardeners were employed, and often the upkeep of the tomb was provided from the income realised from the sale of vegetables, fruit, and flowers grown there.

The famous mausoleum at Corbridge had an enclosing wall which formed a precinct 134 feet square. It was almost certainly laid to lawn, but it is possible that the area was also planted with shrubs and flower beds. Pollen analysis would confirm this.

Less elaborate tombs were simply planted with single trees, groups of shrubs, or flower beds.

Tombs and cemeteries were most often situated along the roads outside of towns. Such a cemetery dating from the 3rd century flanked the road approaching Bremenium (Watling Street near High Rochester). At the roadside in front of these cemeteries flowers and fruit could be purchased.

Many tombs, with their orchards and gardens, were purchased for the repose of an entire family or dynasty.

Funerary wreaths and bouquets were a feature of the service for the dead and, in consequence, some plants, herbs, and flowers became associated with death. Their presence in the house of the living was regarded with superstitious dread.

The upkeep of Garden Tombs was paid for by selling fruit, vegetables and flowers

THE GARDEN IN ROMAN BRITAIN

The archaeology of the garden is a recent development. Until a few years ago, archaeologists did not pay much attention to the possibility of the existence of formal gardens attached to villas and houses in Roman Britain. Now, even old excavation reports are being re-examined for evidence that was previously overlooked or misinterpreted.

When the villa at Apethorpe in Northamptonshire was excavated in 1859, a shallow stone-lined depression was found in the exact centre of the courtyard. This was interpreted as an impluvium (a basin for catching rainwater) or a "dipping well". It now seems much more likely that it was a garden feature like an ornamental pool.

A paved path and low scarps which were the remains of terraces were found in the forecourt of the villa at Sudeley in Gloucestershire.

Long narrow structures on two sides of the courtyard at Pitney villa in Somerset are now thought to have been garden pavilions.

Traces of a garden dating from the early 4th century AD were found in front of the villa at Frocester in Gloucestershire. It had rectangular flower beds and bedding trenches for a hedge. The charred remains of box were found. Remains of box were also discovered at Farmoor villa in Oxfordshire.

The foundations of a semicircular structure were found at Brading Villa on the Isle of Wight. This may have been a seated alcove.

Aerial photography in Britain has enabled archaeologists to determine the layouts of buried Roman villa gardens. "Crop marks" show up the outlines of hedge lines and formal planting. Pollen analysis from these gardens is giving us a clearer picture of the types of plants, herbs, and flowers grown in Roman Britain.

An impressive recreation of the gardens of the Romano-British palace of Fishbourne (near Chichester in West Sussex) followed highly disciplined excavations carried out in the 1960s.

Fishbourne Palace is one of the most spectacular Roman buildings to be seen in Britain. It is thought that it was built for the client king, Cogidubnus, as a reward for his pro-Roman sympathy at the time of the Claudian invasion. Archaeological evidence points to a date not earlier than 73 AD for its construction. It was finally destroyed by fire in the late 3rd century AD.

In the centre of the palace complex was a large formal garden laid to lawns surrounded by hedging. Conifers and shrubs formed focal points. There is evidence for trellises and fountains. The form and decoration of the palace reflects the highly sophisticated Mediterranean taste.

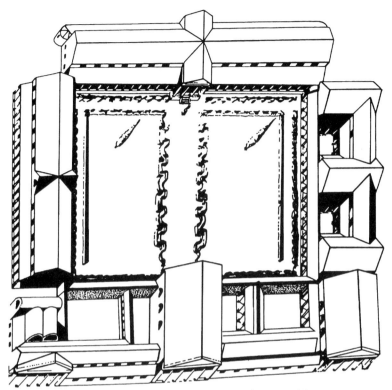

Gardens at Fishbourne Palace

The Corinium Museum has recreated a Roman garden. It is arranged around a central pond. Bedding areas exhibit plants typical of the Roman period. It is proposed that, as the garden matures, new features will be added. The feel of the small town house garden is conveyed by the enclosing space which has decorated walls.

Chedworth Roman Villa has been landscaped and a fine model in the site's reception area conveys strongly its vanished splendour.

It was the ambition of town dwellers to own a place in the country. The Romans loved the outdoor life even if Britain's climate, as one Roman traveller recorded, "is objectionable with frequent rains and mists".

The ideal situation for a country retreat took advantage of views of valleys, mountains, or the sea. It was often surrounded by woodlands and lakes. The hilly, woodland setting of Chedworth is breathtakingly beautiful.

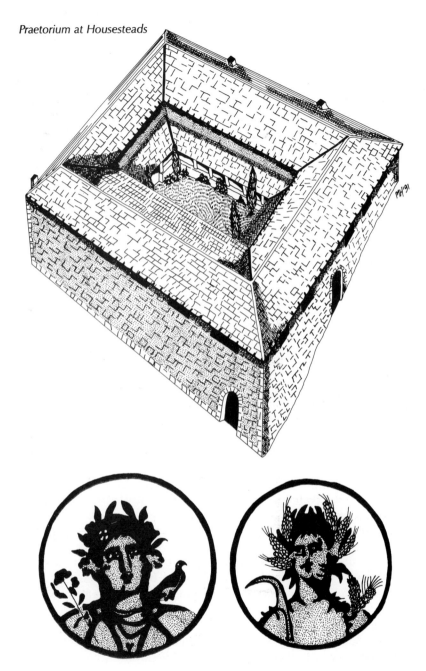

Praetorium at Housesteads

The 'Four Seasons' Mosaic at the Corinium Museum depicts Flora and Ceres

The typical Roman house (Insula) was built in the courtyard style. In the towns this permitted a great deal of privacy and insulation against the worst of the noise from the streets outside.

Pliny the Younger's white marble bedroom opened onto his garden: "There you can lie and imagine you are in a wood, but without the risk of rain! Here I can enjoy a profounder peace, more comfort, and fewer cares. I need never wear a formal toga, and there are no neighbours to disturb me".

From the front entrance to the Roman house one generally walked directly into the atrium, the central court. The other rooms of the house were grouped around and opened onto this. Further ranges of rooms at the rear were grouped around the peristyle, a colonnaded garden court. Some mansions and palaces also had a sunken garden called a hippodromus.

The Mediterranean style was not followed in Britain, probably because of the climate. The Gaulish fashion was followed.

Villas and houses in Roman Britain often had rooms that opened onto one another, rather than directly onto a courtyard. Most villas occupied only one, two, or three sides of a square or rectangle. The path from the main gate led directly up to the main reception room through a landscaped forecourt or formal garden.

The central court of the Mediterranean style of dwelling frequently had a pool or fountain in its centre. Pots and troughs contained plants and shrubs and flower beds, set into the pavements, contained herbs and flowers.

After the Roman forts achieved a permanence in stone, doubtless, the military strived to provide as much in the way of "home" comforts as possible. The courtyard of the commander's house may have had a formal garden. It would be interesting to see the results of the pollen analysis of these areas.

Plants and Flowers in Roman Britain

As well as the sweet scented, flowering herbs that graced their garden beds (see ROMAN HERBAL by Michael Hoadley), the Romans introduced and cultivated a number of flowers, plants, and shrubs. This number is not as great as tradition would have us believe, but it is possible that they also made use of indigenous plants and wild flowers.

Acanthus
(Acanthus mollis)

The Acanthus has glossy green leaves and purple and white flowers. It blooms in July and August and reaches a height of between three and five feet.

The plant inspired the decoration at the top of Corinthian columns. According to the legend, Callimachus (late 5th century BC), the architect, was building a temple at Corinth. He saw the plant growing from under a basket on which a tile had been placed. The leaves had grown right through the basketwork and turned themselves back on the tile. This gave the architect the inspiration for his design. Well, it could have happened!

The Acanthus is quite easy to grow. The quickest method is to take root cuttings in the winter, or divide the roots and replant them in the dormant season. Seed can be sown in the spring or autumn in trays. The seedlings can be planted out in two years' time. Winter protection by means of straw or peat is essential.

The Acanthus likes a partially shaded or sunny position in deep, well-drained soil. It doesn't like to be moved around.

Box
(Buxus)

Box is a hardy shrub of the order Euphorbiaceae. It has thick oval leaves which are dark green on top and a lighter shade underneath.

The flowers appear in small, greenish-yellow clusters in May. It does not flower if it is clipped.

Box seldom grows to a height of more than about 15 feet. It lends itself to shaping and clipping and has been used, at least since Roman times, for ornamental hedges and topiary.

Box can be propagated from cuttings. It is quite slow to grow.

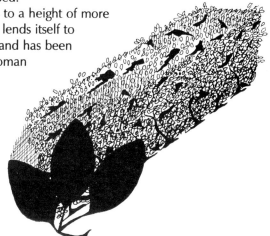

DAFFODIL
(Narcissus pseudonarcissus)

This is a Wild Daffodil, or Lent Lily. It is Britain's only native Daffodil. It is pale yellow and flowers in March and April. It grows to a height of 8-14 inches. In the wild, it is restricted to damp woods and grassland.

The hybridized descendants of the Wild Daffodil will grow anywhere, but do best in organically rich, moist soil. If they do not get enough moisture they may not flower next year.

Daffodil bulbs should be planted in the autumn at least three times the depth of the bulb. Congested plants can be divided out every few years in July. Planting from seed can be slow and disappointing. Diseased plants should be dug up and burned to prevent the spread of viruses.

LAVENDER
(Lavendula officinalis)

Lavender was originally native to the mountainous districts bordering the Western Mediterranean. It can grow at altitudes of up to 4500 feet above sea-level. It prefers stony ground and an open, sunny position. It is cultivated as far north as Norway.

Lavender forms an evergreen undershrub about two feet high. It has greyish-green linear leaves and pale to dark violet flowers.

Propagation is from root division or slips.

MADONNA LILY
(Lilium candidum)

This is a hardy lily with a very strong, sweet scent. The flower is pure white and blooms in June and July. It grows to a height of four to five feet.

The Madonna Lily is thought to be the oldest cultivated flower. It was known to the Assyrians and the Phoenicians. It is depicted on Minoan vases dating from before 1600 BC. It was noted for its curative powers: it was used to treat dropsy and boils.

The Roman Army planted it near their permanent forts because of its reputation for curing corns: no doubt a problem on long marches.

The Madonna Lily is not the easiest plant to grow. It is often attacked by Lily virus (Botrytis). Bulbs should be planted in shallow, slightly alkaline soil, with the top of the bulb just above the level of the soil. This should be done no later than the beginning of September. Seeds can be sown deeply in pots in the early autumn and protected until mature.

MULBERRY
(Morus spp.)

The Mulberry was brought
to Britain by the Romans. It
is a short, squat tree with a
broad, rounded crown. It has
heart-shaped leaves that have toothed
edges. The trees are either male or female:
the male being rare in Britain.

The female trees have oval catkins of crowded
green flowers. In the summer, these catkins swell
and turn crimson. They form berries with a single hard seed and juicy
pulp. The berries are purple or black when ripe and make an excellent
jam. The Romans used them in cooking.

The male Mulberry bears hanging green catkins in May. These
contain many tiny, four-petalled flowers.

The Mulberry is propagated by tip layering. It is slow to grow and
rarely exceeds 30 feet in height, but it can live for up to 150 years.

MYRTLE
(Myrtus communis)

According to the legend the Roman goddess of
love, Venus, wore a Myrtle crown when she
rose from the sea. Hence, the association of
the plant with love and with brides.

The plant was very probably introduced
into Britain by the Romans in the 1st
century. There is a great deal of
tradition and folklore attached to the
plant and it has links with Roman art
and architecture, as has the Acanthus.

Myrtle is an evergreen shrub with
fragrant white flowers. It can grow up to
15 feet in height. It flowers in July and
August. The leaves are aromatic when crushed.

The plant is not the hardiest and requires protection. It can be grown
in large pots and be put out during the summer. It will thrive in a
sheltered position. The leaves are tough and resist garden pests.

Myrtle can be propagated by taking short cuttings of lateral shoots
taken in the summer.

Opium Poppy
(Papaver somniferum)

The Opium Poppy is a highly ornamental plant that grows to a height of two and a half feet. Colour varies from mauve to red to pink and white. It flowers from June to August. Alas, the smell is not very pleasant.

It was native to the Middle East and the Mediterranean. It came to Britain with the Romans: probably as a weed seed in fodder or on the hooves of their horses. The Romans used it as a narcotic and as an anaesthetic in medicine, though it was regarded as dangerous.

The plant is very easy to grow, but it can become a destructive weed in flower borders. It is not fussy, but enjoys a sunny position.

Pansy
(Viola spp).

The pansy is a perennial herb of the order violaceae. The name is generally given to the garden flower; the wild pansy being called heartsease. The heartsease (Viola tricolor) is a native of Britain. The pansy is related to the violet.

The leaves of the pansy have rounded lobes and the flowers are blue-violet yellow, creamy-white or a combination of these colours. The pansy blooms from April to September.

Heartsease is a cornfield weed and has blue-violet flowers; a yellow form can be found growing in dunes and grassland near the sea. The field pansy (Viola arvensis) has smaller flowers than heartsease and can be found growing in arable fields and waste lands.

ROSES
(Rosa spp.)

There is not sufficient space here for a subject to which whole volumes have been devoted.

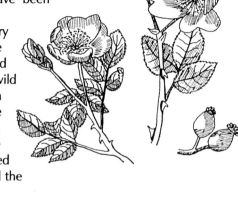

The Romans were very fond of roses. There are more than 1000 cultivated species and over 100 wild varieties have been identified in Britain. Of the wild varieties the downy, the dog, the burnet, the field, and the apple-scented are the most common and the most easily recognised.

The Romans believed that the Dog Rose could cure hydrophobia – it can't!

The cultivated varieties in English gardens have all evolved from wild originals. Rosa gallica probably came to Britain with the Romans.

Roses are propagated from seed, cuttings, layering, budding, and grafting.

The Romans used rose petals in cooking. Roses were also used in the preparation of medicines. They appear in Roman art and as an architectural motif.

The Emperor Nero ordered a million roses for a winter banquet.

VIOLETS
(Viola spp.)

The violet is actually a herb. Ten species grow wild in Britain. The Romans were partial to the Sweet Violet, which has a distinctive odour.

It is a spring flowering plant, but sometimes it flowers again in the autumn. All of the species have more or less heart-shaped leaves. They have blue, violet, and, less commonly, white flowers. They grow in a variety of soils and conditions.

The Sweet Violet has a regular form and is self-pollinating. It produces seeds. It does not attract the interest of insects.

King Cogidubnus in his garden at Fishbourne

28

FISHBOURNE PALACE AND ITS GARDEN

Just outside of Chichester (Roman Noviomagus) in Sussex stood one of the most impressive buildings to have been erected in Roman Britain. This was the Palace of Fishbourne.

It has not been established beyond all doubt just who owned Fishbourne Palace, but the principal candidate is Cogidubnus, King of the Regnenses. This tribe was staunchly pro-Roman and the Palace may have been a reward to the king for his support. The early date (building may have begun in the 60s AD) and its lavish appearance indicate official subsidy for its construction. It has also been suggested that Fishbourne served as a seaside residence for the provincial governor.

Although not a villa in the normal sense, the Palace had many of the characteristics of the villa maritima (seaside estate).

The Palace was constructed around a large central courtyard within which was a carefully laid out ornamental garden. The entrance to the Palace was in the east wing through an imposing colonnaded hall that gave in directly to the garden. Rooms led off on the north side and were arranged around small porticoed courtyards. A similar arrangement made up the north wing. Between the east wing and the north wing, in the corner, was a large aisled hall. The west wing, directly opposite the entrance, had a set of steps leading up from the garden to the audience chamber. Here, seated in state, the king could observe all who crossed the garden to seek an audience with him. Other rooms served as offices and reception rooms. A covered private walkway was built behind the west wing. The south side of the Palace is under the modern road. This was probably the royal residence and may have faced onto a private garden with the sea beyond. The royal bath suite was in the southeast corner. The north wing of the Palace alone comprised of 23 rooms.

The mosaics at Fishbourne are world famous. They include early geometric black and white mosaics and a third century marine mosaic with a boy riding a dolphin in its central roundel (it is edged round with aquatic and plant motifs).

Excavations at the Palace revealed the bedding trenches of the garden. The half-round basin of a fountain was unearthed and evidence of trellises was revealed. The remains of root systems were traced and pollen analysis revealed the presence of opium poppy. Fresh farm loam had been turned into the garden when it was being planted out. Espalier (fan trellises) planting had been done against the Palace walls. Lawned areas had been surrounded by box hedging.

More than 20 years ago the garden was replanted. Central areas were relaid to lawn surrounded by hedging in geometric patterns. The established formal garden suggests the appearance of the Palace in Roman times, but it lacks the water features for which there was considerable evidence. In Roman times a conduit ran diagonally across the garden from a header tank to a pool in one corner which provided water for the garden.

Recently, a research garden has been established in which a variety of herbs, food plants and other plants for study are being cultivated.

★   ★   ★   ★   ★

In 410AD, the Emperor Honorius wrote to Britain to say that the Province could no longer depend on Rome's protection and support. Roman Britain disintegrated and, along with the other cultural advantages of Romanisation, the formal garden disappeared.

Formal gardens of any description did not reappear in Britain until after the Norman Conquest. From the 18th century down to the present, Roman horticultural concepts have exerted a strong influence on garden design.

> *"This is one of my prayers: for a*
> *parcel of land not so very large,*
> *which should have a garden..."*
> —Horace

> *"As a flower grows concealed in an*
> *enclosed garden, unknown to cattle,*
> *bruised by no plough, which the*
> *breezes caress, the sun makes strong,*
> *and the rain brings out..."*
> —Catullus

The Garden Pool

The Garden of Victory